Never Divide The Disparity.
Negotiating As Though It Were Your Last.

Vana Hendy

ISBN:9798884251823

Dedication

With the help of Almighty God who
lives forever,I dedicate this work to all

who sees the need to do the right thing
at the right time;YOU.

CONTENTS

Acknowledgments i

1 BEND THEIR REALITY: 1
Shape what is Fair

2 THE NEW RULE: 16
Becoming the Smartest Person

3 DON'T FEEL THEIR PAIN: Navigating Empathy in Bridging Disparities   28

4 BARGAIN HARD: Negotiating Equity   35

5 NAVIGATING THE DICHOTOMY OF   53

"YES" AND "NO" IN THE PURSUIT OF EQUITY

6 ACHIEVING WIN-WIN OUTCOMES: 63

Applying the "Never Divide the Disparity" Principle

7 EMBRACING 74

DIALOGUE
OVER
ARGUMEN
TATION

8 CULTIVATI 80
NG
INSTANT
LIKEABILIT
Y
THROUGH
UNITY
AND
UNDERST
ANDING

9 EMBRACIN 97
G
CONSTRU

CTIVE CRITICISM WITH COMPASSION AND UNDERSTANDING

10 EMBRACING 110 G UNCERTAINTY AND HUMILITY:

Setting Boundaries

11 About the author

Never Divide The Disparity.

130

ACKNOWLEDGMENTS

I would like to express my heartfelt gratitude to the individuals who have played a significant role in the realization of this book. Their support, guidance, and encouragement have been invaluable.

First and foremost, I extend my deepest thanks to Almighty God for his love and mercy,I also want to thank my family and friends for their expertise, inspiration, encouragement.Your wisdom, insights, motivation significantly enriched this project.

I am also grateful to My Lecturers for their editorial assistance, feedback, support during challenging times.Your keen eye and thoughtful suggestions have greatly enhanced the quality of this work.

A special thanks to my mentor for his technical assistance and research support. Your dedication and expertise were instrumental in bringing this book to fruition.

Finally, a heartfelt thank you to my readers. Your interest in my work is the ultimate reward, and I am truly grateful for the opportunity to share this story with you.

Thank you all for being a part of this journey.

Sincerely,

Vana Hendy.

1 BEND THEIR REALITY

In the grand tapestry of human existence, woven into the fabric of society, lies a stark and undeniable truth: Disparity. It is a multifaceted phenomenon, manifesting in various forms across the globe, casting shadows of inequality, injustice, and imbalance. From the economic chasms cleaving communities apart to the socio-cultural divides that perpetuate prejudice, disparity stands as a formidable barrier to progress and unity.

Yet, amid the darkness of this disparity, there exists a glimmer of hope——a beacon that illuminates the path towards a more equitable world. It is the notion of bending reality, of defying the limitations imposed by disparity, and forging a new paradigm of inclusivity and understanding. But to embark on this transformative journey, one must first grasp the intricacies of disparity and recognize its pervasive influence on every aspect of human life.

At its core, disparity encompasses a wide array of dimensions. Economic inequality, perhaps the most palpable manifestation, delineates the chasm between the affluent and the impoverished, shaping access to resources, opportunities, and basic necessities. In a world where wealth begets power and privilege, millions languish in the shadows of poverty, their aspirations stifled by the suffocating grip of financial deprivation.

Yet, the specter of disparity extends beyond the realm of economics, permeating social structures and cultural norms with its divisive touch. Racial and ethnic disparities, ingrained through centuries of systemic oppression and prejudice, perpetuate discrimination and marginalization, erecting barriers to equality and justice. Gender disparities, likewise, consign women to subordinate roles, constraining their autonomy and impeding their pursuit of empowerment and self-determination.

Moreover, disparaging disparities manifest in the realms of education, healthcare, and environmental sustainability, further exacerbating the inequities that plague our world. Educational disparities deny countless individuals the transformative power of knowledge, relegating them to the sidelines of progress and development. Healthcare disparities condemn the vulnerable and marginalized to inferior medical care, exacerbating health outcomes and perpetuating cycles of suffering and despair. Environmental disparities, in turn, disproportionately burden marginalized communities with the brunt of environmental degradation and climate change, amplifying their vulnerability to ecological crises.

In the face of such formidable challenges, the imperative to bend reality becomes increasingly urgent. It requires a concerted effort to challenge the status quo, dismantle entrenched systems of oppression, and nurture a collective consciousness of empathy and solidarity. It demands innovative solutions and bold interventions that transcend conventional boundaries and bridge the chasms of disparity with the bonds of equality and justice.

Yet, bending reality is not merely an act of defiance—it is a testament to the resilience and indomitable spirit of humanity. It is a declaration of our shared humanity, our inherent worth, and our capacity to transcend the limitations imposed by disparity. It is a call to action, echoing through the corridors of history, beckoning us to rise above our differences and strive towards a world where every individual is afforded the opportunity to flourish and thrive.

In this pursuit, we are not without guides. History presents us with luminaries who dared to challenge the status quo, who refused to accept the world as it was handed to them. Their stories serve as beacons of inspiration, illuminating the path forward with their unwavering commitment to justice and equality.

Consider the legacy of Nelson Mandela, who, in the face of insurmountable odds, steadfastly opposed apartheid in South Africa, refusing to compromise his principles in the pursuit of freedom. His resilience, his unwavering belief in the power of reconciliation, stands as a testament to the transformative potential of forgiveness and understanding.

Or reflect on the tireless advocacy of Malala Yousafzai, who, despite facing threats to her life, courageously championed the right to education for girls in Pakistan and around the world. Her unwavering determination, her unyielding commitment to equality, serves as a reminder that even the smallest voices can spark the flames of change.

These trailblazers, and countless others like them, remind us that the journey to bend reality is not for the faint of heart. It requires courage in the face of adversity, perseverance in the midst of despair, and an unwavering commitment to the principles of justice and equality.

But it is a journey worth embarking on, for in bending reality, we not only transform the world around us, but we also transform ourselves. We shed the shackles of apathy and indifference, embracing our shared humanity with empathy and compassion. We cultivate a spirit of solidarity, recognizing that our destinies are intertwined, and that true progress can only be achieved through collective action.

So let us embark on this journey with open hearts and open minds, guided by the principles of justice, equality, and empathy. Let us bend reality, not to conform to the whims of the powerful, but to create a world where every individual has the opportunity to thrive. And let us never forget that in the struggle against disparity, our greatest strength lies in our unity, our solidarity, and our unwavering belief in the inherent dignity of every human being.

For it is in unity that we find our strength, and it is in solidarity that we find our hope. Together, let us bend reality and bridge disparities, forging a brighter future for generations to come.

Shape what is Fair

Fairness, at its essence, embodies the idea of equity—the notion that every individual should be afforded the same opportunities, rights, and dignity, regardless of their background or circumstances. Yet, achieving equity is no simple task, as it requires a nuanced understanding of the myriad factors that contribute to disparity and injustice.

One fundamental aspect of shaping fairness lies in dismantling the barriers that perpetuate inequality. This entails confronting systemic injustices head-on, whether they manifest as discriminatory policies, institutional biases, or socio-economic disparities. It requires a commitment to challenging the status quo, disrupting entrenched power structures, and amplifying the voices of the marginalized and oppressed.

Moreover, shaping fairness necessitates a reevaluation of our societal values and priorities. It requires us to question the narratives that justify inequality and privilege, and to cultivate a culture of inclusivity and empathy. It entails recognizing the inherent worth and dignity of every individual, regardless of their race, gender, sexual orientation, or socio-economic status, and actively working to dismantle the prejudices and stereotypes that perpetuate discrimination.

Education plays a pivotal role in shaping fairness, serving as a catalyst for social change and empowerment. By ensuring equitable access to quality education for all, we equip individuals with the tools they need to challenge injustice, pursue their aspirations, and contribute meaningfully to society. Moreover, education fosters empathy and understanding, cultivating a generation of empathetic leaders who are committed to creating a more equitable world.

In addition to education, equitable access to healthcare is essential for shaping fairness. Healthcare is a fundamental human right, yet millions around the world are denied access to essential medical services due to socio-economic disparities, discrimination, and inadequate healthcare infrastructure. By advocating for universal healthcare coverage and addressing the root causes of health disparities, we can ensure that everyone has the opportunity to lead healthy and fulfilling lives.

Furthermore, shaping fairness requires a commitment to environmental justice. Climate change and environmental degradation disproportionately impact marginalized communities, exacerbating existing disparities and perpetuating cycles of poverty and injustice. By prioritizing environmental sustainability and advocating for policies that promote equitable access to clean air, water, and natural resources, we can create a more just and sustainable future for all.

Ultimately, shaping what is fair requires collective action and solidarity. It demands that we come together as a global community to confront the injustices that divide us and to build a world where every individual has the opportunity to thrive. By embracing the principles of equity, empathy, and justice, we can bend reality to bridge disparities and create a brighter and more equitable future for generations to come.

2 THE NEW RULE

In the quest to bridge disparities and reshape our world into a more equitable and just place, a new rule emerges—one that transcends traditional notions of intelligence and success. This rule is not about individual achievement or superiority, but rather about collective empowerment and solidarity. It is a rule that challenges us to redefine what it means to be "smart" and to recognize that true wisdom lies in our ability to work together to overcome the barriers that divide us.

The first tenet of this new rule is

empathy—the ability to understand and share the feelings of others. Empathy is not just a soft skill; it is a fundamental aspect of human connection and solidarity. By empathizing with those who experience the brunt of inequality and injustice, we can better understand the root causes of disparity and work towards meaningful solutions that address the needs of all members of society.

The second tenet is humility—the recognition that none of us has all the answers, and that true wisdom comes from a willingness to listen and learn from others. In a world plagued by division and polarization, humility allows us to set aside our egos and engage in dialogue with those whose perspectives may differ from our own. It is through humble collaboration and exchange of ideas that we can uncover innovative solutions to complex problems.

The third tenet is courage—the willingness to confront injustice and advocate for change, even in the face of adversity. Courage is not the absence of fear, but rather the ability to act in spite of it. It is the courage to speak out against discrimination, to challenge oppressive systems, and to stand up for the rights of the marginalized and oppressed. It is through acts of courage that we can bend reality and create a more just and equitable world.

The fourth tenet is resilience—the ability to persevere in the face of setbacks and obstacles. Building a more equitable society will not be easy, and there will undoubtedly be challenges along the way. But it is through resilience—through our ability to bounce back from adversity and keep pushing forward—that we can overcome these challenges and continue our journey towards a brighter future.

Finally, the fifth tenet is solidarity—the recognition that we are all in this together, and that our fates are intertwined. Solidarity means standing shoulder to shoulder with those who are most affected by inequality and injustice, and working together to build a more inclusive and equitable world. It is through solidarity that we can bridge the divides that separate us and create a future where everyone has the opportunity to thrive.

In implementing the new rule on "Never Divide the Disparity," it becomes apparent that true intelligence is not solely measured by academic prowess or intellectual acumen, but by our capacity for empathy, humility, courage, resilience, and solidarity. These qualities serve as the foundation upon which we can build a more equitable and just society, transcending the barriers of disparity that divide us.

Empathy allows us to connect with others on a deeper level, understanding their experiences and perspectives, and fostering a sense of compassion and understanding. It enables us to recognize the humanity in each individual, regardless of their background or circumstances, and motivates us to take action to address the injustices they face.

Humility reminds us that we are all fallible beings, capable of making mistakes and learning from our experiences. It encourages us to approach the complex issues of inequality and injustice with an open mind, willing to listen to diverse viewpoints and collaborate with others to find solutions that benefit everyone.

Courage emboldens us to speak truth to power, to challenge the status quo, and to confront injustice wherever it may arise. It requires us to step outside our comfort zones and take risks in the pursuit of a more equitable world, knowing that the path to progress is often fraught with obstacles and resistance.

Resilience sustains us in the face of adversity, enabling us to persevere through setbacks and challenges on our journey towards justice. It empowers us to pick ourselves up after each defeat, to learn from our failures, and to continue fighting for what we believe in with renewed determination and resolve.

Solidarity binds us together as a collective force for change, reminding us that our struggles are interconnected and that we are stronger when we stand united. It inspires us to work collaboratively with others, across lines of difference, to build coalitions and movements that amplify the voices of the marginalized and oppressed.

As we continue to implement the new rule on "Never Divide the Disparity," it becomes increasingly clear that the journey towards justice and equity is not linear. It is a path filled with twists and turns, victories and setbacks, but guided by the principles of empathy, humility, courage, resilience, and solidarity, we can navigate this journey with purpose and determination.

One crucial aspect of this journey is the need for continuous learning and growth. True intelligence lies not in static knowledge, but in our willingness to question, to listen, and to adapt in response to new information and experiences. By remaining open to feedback and new perspectives, we can refine our understanding of the issues at hand and refine our strategies for creating meaningful change.

Moreover, as we work towards bridging disparities and reshaping our world into a more just and equitable place, we must remain vigilant against the forces of division and injustice that seek to undermine our progress. This requires us to be proactive in challenging discrimination, oppression, and systemic inequalities wherever they may arise, and to stand firm in our commitment to justice and solidarity.

Additionally, it is essential to recognize the importance of intersectionality in our efforts towards equity. Intersectionality reminds us that individuals experience oppression and privilege in complex, overlapping ways, shaped by factors such as race, gender, class, sexuality, and ability. By taking an intersectional approach to our work, we can better understand the interconnected nature of inequality and develop solutions that address the unique needs of all members of society.

Furthermore, as we strive to bridge disparities and create a more equitable world, it is essential to center the voices and experiences of those most affected by injustice. This means actively seeking out and amplifying the perspectives of marginalized communities, and ensuring that they have a seat at the table in decision-making processes that affect their lives.

let us remember that true intelligence is not measured by how much we know, but by how we use our knowledge and skills to create a more just and equitable world for all. By embodying empathy, humility, courage, resilience, and solidarity, we can become the smartest person on the journey towards justice, bending reality to bridge the disparities that divide us and forging a brighter future for generations to come.

Ultimately, the journey towards justice and equity is one that requires collective effort and sustained commitment. By embracing the new rule on "Never Divide the Disparity" and embodying the principles of empathy, humility, courage, resilience, and solidarity, we can become agents of positive change in our communities and beyond. Together, let us continue to bend reality and bridge the disparities that divide us, forging a future where fairness, quality, and justice are not just ideals, but lived realities for all

3 DON'T FEEL THEIR PAIN

In our pursuit of bridging disparities and fostering a more equitable society, empathy stands as a powerful tool for understanding and connecting with others. Yet, amidst the urgency of addressing injustice, there exists a delicate balance between empathizing with those who experience disparity and preserving our own emotional well-being. In this chapter, we explore the nuances of empathy and the importance of maintaining boundaries as we navigate the complexities of bridging disparities.

Empathy, at its core, is the ability to understand and share the feelings of others. It allows us to connect on a human level, to recognize the experiences and struggles of those around us, and to respond with compassion and solidarity. However, as we immerse ourselves in the stories of others, it is crucial to recognize the potential toll that empathy can take on our own emotional health.

The title, "Never Divide the Disparity," serves as a reminder that while we strive to bridge the gaps that divide us, we must also safeguard against allowing those divisions to consume us emotionally. This means setting boundaries and practicing self-care to prevent burnout and compassion fatigue, particularly when confronting the deep-seated injustices that perpetuate disparity.

One way to navigate empathy while bridging disparities is to cultivate a sense of compassionate detachment. This involves maintaining a level of emotional distance from the pain and suffering of others, while still remaining engaged and committed to addressing injustice. By striking a balance between empathy and detachment, we can remain empathetic without becoming overwhelmed by the weight of others' experiences.

Furthermore, it is essential to recognize that empathy does not require us to directly experience the pain of others in order to understand

and support them. While empathy involves acknowledging and validating the emotions of others, it is also possible to empathize from a place of relative privilege, without fully comprehending the depth of someone else's suffering.

In addition, practicing empathy involves active listening and validation, rather than trying to fix or solve the problems of others. By creating space for individuals to share their experiences and feelings without judgment or interference, we can foster a sense of trust and connection that is essential for meaningful dialogue and collaboration.

However, as we navigate empathy in the journey to bridge disparities, it's important to acknowledge that empathy alone is not sufficient to drive meaningful change. While empathy allows us to understand and connect with the experiences of others, it must be coupled with action to address the root causes of disparity and injustice.

This underscores the significance of moving beyond empathy towards allyship and advocacy. Allyship involves actively standing in solidarity with marginalized communities, amplifying their voices, and working alongside them to dismantle oppressive systems. It requires a commitment to challenging privilege, advocating for policy changes, and using our own platforms and resources to uplift those who are marginalized.

Moreover, effective advocacy requires an intersectional approach that recognizes the interconnected nature of inequality and oppression. This means acknowledging that individuals experience disparity differently based on their intersecting identities and addressing the unique challenges faced by marginalized groups. By centering the voices of those most affected by injustice, we can develop more inclusive and effective solutions that address the root causes of disparity.

Additionally, it's important to recognize the limitations of empathy and allyship and to actively work towards dismantling the systems of power and privilege that perpetuate inequality. This may involve confronting our own biases and privileges, engaging in difficult conversations, and challenging oppressive structures within our own communities and institutions.

Furthermore, as we navigate empathy and allyship in the pursuit of justice, it's essential to prioritize self-care and collective care. This means recognizing that the work of bridging disparities can be emotionally taxing and committing to supporting one another in our collective efforts. By fostering a culture of care and mutual support, we can sustain our activism and resilience over the long term.

In conclusion, while empathy is a powerful tool for understanding and connecting with others, it must be coupled with action to drive meaningful change. By moving beyond empathy towards allyship, advocacy, and collective action, we can work together to dismantle the systems of inequality and create a more just and equitable world for all. As we continue on this journey, let us remain committed to bridging disparities with empathy, intentionality, and a shared vision of justice   and   solidarity.

4 BARGAIN HARD

In the intricate dance of bridging disparities, negotiation emerges as a pivotal tool for advocating for equity and justice. The title, "Never Divide the Disparity," encapsulates the ethos of this chapter, reminding us of the imperative to remain steadfast in our commitment to unity and solidarity, even as we navigate the complexities of negotiation.

Negotiation is not simply about securing the best deal for oneself; rather, it is about finding common ground, building consensus, and working towards mutually beneficial outcomes. In the context of bridging disparities, negotiation involves navigating power dynamics, addressing conflicting interests, and advocating for solutions that address the needs of all stakeholders.

One crucial aspect of negotiation is the need for transparency and accountability. Transparency ensures that all parties have access to relevant information and are able to make informed decisions, while accountability holds individuals and institutions responsible for their actions and commitments. By prioritizing transparency and accountability in negotiations, we can foster trust and build stronger partnerships for change.

Moreover, negotiation requires a willingness to listen and compromise, even in the face of disagreement. It involves seeking common ground and finding creative solutions that address the underlying causes of disparity, rather than simply treating the symptoms. By engaging in constructive dialogue and collaboration, we can overcome barriers and forge pathways towards equity and justice.

However, it's important to recognize that negotiation is not without its challenges. Power imbalances, entrenched interests, and systemic inequalities can all complicate the negotiation process and hinder progress towards equitable outcomes. In these situations, it becomes essential to advocate for the rights and needs of marginalized communities, while also recognizing the importance of building alliances and coalitions to amplify our collective voice.

As we continue to bargain hard for equity within the framework of "Never Divide the Disparity," it's essential to recognize that negotiation is not a one-size-fits-all process. Different contexts, stakeholders, and issues may require different approaches and strategies. However, regardless of the specifics, there are certain principles and practices that can guide our negotiation efforts towards more equitable outcomes.

One such principle is the importance of centering the voices and experiences of marginalized communities in the negotiation process. Too often, decisions are made without meaningful input from those who are most affected by disparity and injustice. By actively seeking out and amplifying the perspectives of marginalized groups, we can ensure that our negotiation efforts are rooted in the realities and needs of those they aim to benefit.

Another crucial aspect of negotiation is the need for intersectional analysis. Recognizing that individuals experience disparity differently based on their intersecting identities—such as race, gender, class, sexuality, and ability—is essential for developing solutions that address the complexities of inequality. By taking an intersectional approach to negotiation, we can better understand the nuances of disparity and advocate for policies and practices that promote equity for all.

Additionally, it's important to approach negotiation with a long-term perspective and a commitment to building relationships and trust over time. Sustainable change often requires building alliances and coalitions, fostering collaboration across sectors and communities, and working towards common goals. By investing in relationships and partnerships, we can create a more robust and resilient movement for equity and justice.

Moreover, negotiation requires a willingness to challenge power dynamics and confront systemic barriers to equity. This may involve advocating for policy reforms, pushing back against institutionalized discrimination, and demanding accountability from those in positions of power. By leveraging our collective voice and advocating for systemic change, we can create an environment that is more conducive to equity and justice for all.

In conclusion, negotiation is a critical

tool for advancing equity and justice in the journey to bridge disparities. By centering marginalized voices, adopting an intersectional analysis, building relationships and trust, and challenging power dynamics, we can negotiate for more equitable outcomes that benefit all members of society. As we continue to bargain hard for equity within the framework of "Never Divide the Disparity," let us remain steadfast in our commitment to building a more just and equitable world for all.

Negotiating Equity

Negotiating equity involves navigating complex power dynamics and advocating for fair and just outcomes that address systemic disparities. Here are some additional insights on negotiating equity and how to get your price.

Understanding Power Dynamics: Power imbalances often shape negotiation processes, with certain individuals or groups wielding more influence and leverage than others.

Recognizing these power dynamics is crucial for ensuring that all stakeholders have an equal voice and are able to participate meaningfully in the negotiation process. This may involve advocating for more inclusive decision-making structures and creating opportunities for marginalized voices to be heard.

Building Coalitions: Negotiating for equity is often more effective when done collectively. Building coalitions with like-minded individuals and organizations can amplify our collective voice and increase our bargaining power. By uniting behind common goals and strategies, we can exert greater pressure on decision-makers and advocate more effectively for systemic change.

Fostering Dialogue and Collaboration:

Effective negotiation requires open and honest dialogue among all stakeholders. Creating opportunities for constructive dialogue and collaboration can help build understanding, trust, and mutual respect among parties with differing perspectives. By fostering a culture of collaboration and partnership, we can work together towards shared goals and find solutions that benefit everyone.

Addressing Structural Inequities: Negotiating equity often involves addressing the root causes of systemic disparities, rather than simply addressing their symptoms. This may require advocating for policy reforms, institutional changes, and investments in programs and initiatives that address structural inequities. By addressing the structural barriers that perpetuate inequality, we can create a more equitable society where everyone has the opportunity to thrive.

Measuring Impact and Holding Accountable: Negotiating equity requires ongoing monitoring and evaluation to assess the impact of our efforts and hold decision-makers accountable for their commitments. This may involve tracking key indicators of progress, soliciting feedback from affected communities, and holding regular check-ins to review and adjust strategies as needed. By holding ourselves and others accountable for advancing equity, we can ensure that our negotiation efforts translate into meaningful change.

Cultivating Empathy and Cultural Competence: Effective negotiation for equity requires a deep understanding of the diverse experiences, perspectives, and needs of all stakeholders involved. Cultivating empathy and cultural competence can help negotiators navigate complex interpersonal dynamics, bridge differences, and build trust across diverse communities. By actively listening to and valuing the voices of those most affected by disparity, we can negotiate more equitable outcomes that reflect the realities and needs of all members of society.

Prepare Thoroughly: Before entering into any negotiation, it's crucial to prepare thoroughly. This includes researching the relevant issues, understanding the interests and priorities of all stakeholders involved, and developing a clear understanding of your own goals and objectives. By being well-informed and prepared, you can enter into negotiations with confidence and a solid understanding of what you hope to achieve.

Establish Your Value Proposition: In any negotiation, it's essential to articulate your value proposition—what you bring to the table and why your perspective or proposal is worth considering. This may involve highlighting your expertise, experience, and unique insights, as well as the potential benefits of your proposal for all parties involved. By clearly articulating your value proposition, you can build credibility and persuade others to consider your perspective.

Set Realistic Goals and Prioritize: While it's important to aim high in negotiations, it's also essential to set realistic goals and prioritize your objectives. Identify the most critical issues or outcomes that you hope to achieve and focus your efforts on those priorities. By setting clear and achievable goals, you can avoid getting bogged down in unproductive debates and maximize your chances of success.

Listen Actively and Build Rapport: Effective negotiation is as much about listening as it is about advocating for your own interests. Actively listen to the perspectives and concerns of other parties, and seek to understand their underlying interests and priorities. Building rapport and establishing trust with other negotiators can help create a more collaborative and productive negotiation environment, increasing the likelihood of reaching a mutually beneficial agreement.

Be Flexible and Creative: Negotiation often requires flexibility and creativity in finding solutions that address the interests and concerns of all parties involved. Be open to exploring alternative approaches and compromises that may not have been initially considered. By being flexible and creative in your negotiation approach, you can increase the likelihood of finding win-win solutions that satisfy everyone's needs.

Use Data and Evidence: Support your arguments and proposals with data, evidence, and compelling arguments. Quantitative data, case studies, and expert opinions can help bolster your position and provide credibility to your arguments. Presenting compelling evidence can help persuade others of the validity of your perspective and increase the likelihood of reaching a favorable outcome.

Be Patient and Persistent:

Negotiation is often a process that requires patience and persistence. Be prepared for setbacks and challenges along the way, and be willing to engage in ongoing dialogue and negotiation to reach a resolution. By remaining patient and persistent in your negotiation efforts, you can increase your chances of achieving your desired outcomes over time.

Know When to Walk Away: While it's important to be flexible and open to compromise in negotiation, it's also essential to know when to walk away from a deal that does not meet your needs or objectives. Establish clear boundaries and red lines, and be prepared to walk away from negotiations that do not align with your principles or values. By knowing when to walk away, you can maintain your integrity and avoid settling for less than you deserve.

In conclusion, negotiating for equity requires a combination of preparation, active listening, flexibility, and persistence. By adopting a strategic and principled approach to negotiation, you can effectively advocate for fair and just outcomes that address systemic disparities and promote equity for all members of society.

5 NAVIGATING THE DICHOTOMY OF "YES" AND "NO" IN THE PURSUIT OF EQUITY

In the intricate landscape of bridging disparities and advocating for equity, the dichotomy of "yes" and "no" presents itself as a multifaceted challenge. The title, "Never Divide the Disparity," encapsulates the underlying ethos of this chapter, emphasizing the importance of navigating this dichotomy with care and intentionality in our pursuit of justice and equality.

"Yes" and "no" are not merely binary responses but rather complex expressions of consent, agreement, and dissent that reflect the intricate dynamics of power, privilege, and agency. Understanding the nuances of these responses is essential for effectively navigating negotiations, fostering collaboration, and advocating for equitable outcomes.

"Yes" often signifies agreement, consent, or affirmation—an acknowledgment of shared goals or objectives. In the context of bridging disparities, "yes" may represent a willingness to collaborate, support, or take action to address systemic injustices. However, it's essential to recognize that not all "yeses" are created equal. Some may be genuine expressions of commitment and solidarity, while others may be superficial or conditional, masking underlying power dynamics or conflicts of interest.

Conversely, "no" often signifies disagreement, dissent, or refusal—a rejection of proposed ideas, policies, or actions. While "no" may initially be perceived as a barrier to progress, it can also serve as a catalyst for deeper reflection, dialogue, and negotiation. By engaging with dissenting voices and exploring the underlying reasons for resistance, we can uncover alternative perspectives and potential areas of compromise that may lead to more equitable outcomes.

However, it's essential to beware the potential pitfalls of the dichotomy of "yes" and "no" in the pursuit of equity. The pressure to secure "yeses" and avoid "nos" may lead to a superficial understanding of complex issues, a reluctance to challenge the status quo, or a failure to acknowledge the perspectives and experiences of marginalized communities. In contrast, an overemphasis on dissent and refusal may result in gridlock, polarization, or the marginalization of minority voices.

Navigating this dichotomy requires a nuanced approach that balances assertiveness with empathy, collaboration with accountability, and resilience with humility. It involves actively listening to diverse perspectives, engaging in constructive dialogue, and seeking common ground while also recognizing and respecting differences of opinion and experience. By fostering a culture of consent, collaboration, and inclusivity, we can navigate the dichotomy of "yes" and "no" in ways that promote equity, justice, and solidarity.

Moreover, it's essential to recognize that genuine progress towards equity often requires challenging the underlying power structures and systemic barriers that perpetuate disparity and injustice. This may involve advocating for policy reforms, institutional changes, and cultural shifts that address the root causes of inequality and promote more equitable outcomes for all members of society.

As we navigate the dichotomy of "yes" and "no" in the pursuit of equity within the framework of "Never Divide the Disparity," it becomes increasingly clear that genuine progress requires a balanced approach that transcends simplistic binaries. Here are some additional considerations and strategies for effectively navigating this dichotomy:

Facilitate Constructive Dialogue: Instead of viewing "yes" and "no" as opposing forces, strive to create spaces for constructive dialogue and collaboration where diverse perspectives can be heard and respected. Encourage open and honest communication, active listening, and the exchange of ideas, even—and especially—when there are disagreements. By fostering a culture of dialogue and mutual respect, we can uncover common ground and identify areas for compromise that promote equitable outcomes.

Seek Consensus, Not Unanimity: While unanimity may be desirable, it's often unrealistic in complex negotiations involving multiple stakeholders with diverse interests and perspectives. Instead of focusing solely on securing "yes" or "no" responses, strive to build consensus around shared values, principles, and objectives. This may involve finding creative solutions that address the needs and concerns of all parties involved, even if they don't result in unanimous agreement.

Empower Marginalized Voices: In the pursuit of equity, it's essential to center the voices and experiences of marginalized communities that are most affected by disparity and injustice. Ensure that decision-making processes are inclusive and participatory, and actively seek out and amplify the perspectives of those who are often marginalized or overlooked. By empowering marginalized voices and prioritizing their needs and concerns, we can create more equitable and inclusive outcomes for all.

Challenge Assumptions and Power Dynamics: Be willing to challenge assumptions, power dynamics, and entrenched interests that may perpetuate disparity and injustice. Question the status quo, interrogate underlying biases, and advocate for changes that promote fairness, equality, and justice. This may involve confronting privilege, addressing systemic barriers, and advocating for policies and practices that promote equity for all members of society.

Practice Resilience and Perseverance: Navigating the dichotomy of "yes" and "no" in the pursuit of equity requires resilience and perseverance in the face of challenges and setbacks. Recognize that progress towards equity is often incremental and non-linear, and be prepared to weather opposition and resistance along the way. Stay committed to your principles and values, and continue to advocate for change, even when the path forward may seem daunting.

In conclusion, navigating the dichotomy of "yes" and "no" in the pursuit of equity requires a nuanced understanding of power dynamics, consent, and agency. By fostering constructive dialogue, seeking consensus, empowering marginalized voices, challenging assumptions and power dynamics, and practicing resilience and perseverance, we can navigate this dichotomy with care and intentionality, advancing towards a future where fairness, equality, and justice are not just ideals but lived realities for all.

6 ACHIEVING WIN-WIN OUTCOMES

In the journey towards equity and justice, the win-win technique serves as a powerful strategy for negotiating outcomes that benefit all parties involved. The title, "Never Divide the Disparity," underscores the importance of finding solutions that bridge divides and promote mutual gain, rather than perpetuating disparities and inequalities. In this chapter, we explore how the win-win technique can be applied within the framework of bridging disparities to achieve equitable and sustainable outcomes.

One of the fundamental principles underpinning the win-win technique is the notion of reframing conflicts as opportunities for collaboration and innovation. Rather than viewing disparities and inequalities as insurmountable obstacles, negotiators employing the win-win approach see them as challenges that can be addressed through creative problem-solving and cooperation. This shift in perspective opens up new possibilities for finding solutions that benefit all parties involved.

Moreover, the win-win technique encourages negotiators to adopt a holistic approach to problem-solving that takes into account the broader context in which disparities exist. Instead of focusing solely on individual transactions or negotiations, this approach considers the underlying systemic factors that perpetuate inequality and injustice. By addressing these root causes, negotiators can develop more comprehensive and sustainable solutions that promote lasting change.

Another key aspect of the win-win technique is the emphasis on communication and collaboration across diverse perspectives and stakeholders. Effective negotiation requires active listening, empathy, and a willingness to engage with differing viewpoints. By creating opportunities for dialogue and collaboration, negotiators can build consensus, forge partnerships, and mobilize collective action to address disparities and promote equity.

Furthermore, the win-win technique recognizes the importance of accountability and transparency in negotiation processes. Negotiators must be accountable to the communities they represent and transparent in their decision-making processes. By operating with integrity and openness, negotiators can build trust and credibility, fostering a more inclusive and participatory negotiation environment.

As negotiators apply the win-win technique within the framework of "Never Divide the Disparity," it's essential to remain vigilant against the forces of division and injustice that seek to undermine progress towards equity and justice. This requires a commitment to challenging power imbalances, confronting privilege, and advocating for policies and practices that promote fairness and equality for all.

In conclusion, the win-win technique offers a powerful approach to negotiation that promotes collaboration, innovation, and equity. By reframing conflicts as opportunities, adopting a holistic approach to problem-solving, fostering communication and collaboration, and prioritizing accountability and transparency, negotiators can work together to address disparities and promote shared prosperity. As we continue to apply the principles of "Never Divide the Disparity" within the context of the win-win technique, let us remain committed to finding solutions that advance equity, justice, and solidarity for all members of society.

Never Divide the Disparity" Principle

The "Never Divide the Disparity" principle serves as a guiding ethos in the pursuit of equity and justice, emphasizing the importance of unity, solidarity, and inclusivity in addressing systemic disparities and inequalities. This principle acknowledges that disparity and division are often rooted in power imbalances, discrimination, and structural inequalities that perpetuate injustice and marginalization. By embracing the "Never Divide the Disparity" principle, individuals and communities commit to working together to bridge divides, amplify marginalized voices, and create a more just and equitable society for all.

At its core, the "Never Divide the Disparity" principle rejects the notion of pitting individuals or groups against each other in a zero-sum game where one's gain comes at the expense of another's loss. Instead, it calls for cooperation, collaboration, and collective action to address the root causes of disparity and promote shared prosperity. This principle recognizes that true progress towards equity requires solidarity across diverse perspectives, identities, and experiences, and that divisions based on race, gender, class, sexuality, and other factors only serve to perpetuate inequality and injustice.

Moreover, the "Never Divide the Disparity" principle challenges individuals and communities to confront their own biases, privileges, and complicity in perpetuating disparity and injustice. It calls for humility, self-reflection, and a willingness to listen and learn from those who are most affected by inequality. By acknowledging and addressing the ways in which systemic disparities manifest in our own lives and communities, we can better understand the interconnected nature of oppression and work towards more inclusive and equitable solutions.

Furthermore, the "Never Divide the Disparity" principle underscores the importance of centering the voices and experiences of marginalized communities in the pursuit of equity and justice. Too often, decisions are made without meaningful input from those who are most affected by disparity and injustice, leading to solutions that fail to address the root causes of inequality. By actively seeking out and amplifying the perspectives of marginalized groups, we can ensure that our efforts towards justice are truly inclusive and equitable.

In practice, the "Never Divide the Disparity" principle informs a wide range of actions and strategies aimed at addressing systemic disparities and promoting equity. This may include advocating for policy reforms that dismantle discriminatory practices and promote inclusive policies, supporting grassroots movements that amplify marginalized voices and challenge power imbalances, and engaging in community organizing efforts that build solidarity and collective power.

Ultimately, the "Never Divide the Disparity" principle reminds us that our struggles for justice and equity are interconnected, and that we must work together to address the root causes of disparity and injustice. By embracing unity, solidarity, and inclusivity, we can build a more just and equitable society where everyone has the opportunity to thrive.

7 EMBRACING DIALOGUE OVER ARGUMENTATION

In the pursuit of equity and justice, the title "Never Divide the Disparity" reminds us of the importance of fostering unity and collaboration, even in the face of disagreement. Chapter Seven delves into the notion that winning arguments does not equate to achieving meaningful progress towards equity. Instead, it advocates for embracing dialogue and understanding as more effective means of addressing systemic disparities.

Arguing often implies a winner and a

loser, a dichotomy that can perpetuate division and hinder progress. In contrast, dialogue fosters mutual understanding, empathy, and collaboration—essential components in the quest for equity. By prioritizing dialogue over argumentation, we can create spaces for meaningful engagement, where diverse perspectives are valued, and collective solutions are sought.

One of the key tenets of dialogue is active listening. Instead of focusing solely on making our own points, we must listen attentively to the perspectives of others, particularly those who have been marginalized or silenced. Active listening requires empathy and openness, as well as a willingness to set aside preconceived notions and biases in order to truly understand the experiences and concerns of others.

Moreover, dialogue encourages curiosity and inquiry, rather than judgment and defensiveness. By approaching conversations with a spirit of curiosity, we can ask questions, seek clarification, and explore differing viewpoints in a respectful and constructive manner. This fosters a culture of learning and growth, where new insights can emerge, and collective understanding can deepen.

In addition, dialogue invites vulnerability and humility, as we acknowledge our own limitations and imperfections. It requires us to recognize that we don't have all the answers and that our perspectives are shaped by our own lived experiences and biases. By embracing vulnerability, we create space for genuine connection and empathy, laying the groundwork for meaningful collaboration and solidarity.

Furthermore, dialogue encourages reflexivity and self-examination, as we interrogate our own privileges and complicity in perpetuating systemic disparities. It challenges us to confront the ways in which our words and actions may inadvertently contribute to inequality and injustice, and to commit to ongoing self-education and growth. This process of self-examination is essential for cultivating the humility and self-awareness necessary for effective allyship and advocacy.

Ultimately, dialogue offers a pathway towards reconciliation and transformation, where disparate voices can come together in pursuit of shared goals and values. By prioritizing dialogue over argumentation, we can create spaces for healing, understanding, and collective action, where the pursuit of equity and justice becomes a collaborative endeavor rather than a battleground of competing interests.

In conclusion, the title "Never Divide the Disparity" reminds us of the importance of prioritizing dialogue over argumentation in the pursuit of equity. By embracing active listening, curiosity, vulnerability, and reflexivity, we can create spaces for meaningful engagement and collaboration, where diverse perspectives are valued, and collective solutions are sought. As we continue on this journey, let us commit to fostering dialogue and understanding as we work towards a more just and equitable society for all.

8 CULTIVATING INSTANT LIKEABILITY THROUGH UNITY AND UNDERSTANDING

In the pursuit of equity and justice encapsulated by the title "Never Divide the Disparity," the ability to cultivate instant likability is not merely a matter of personal charisma or charm. Rather, it is deeply rooted in our capacity to foster unity, empathy, and understanding in our interactions with others. This chapter explores strategies for cultivating instant likability by embracing the principles of unity and understanding within the context of bridging disparities.

Practice Active Listening: One of the most effective ways to instantly connect with others is by practicing active listening. Instead of waiting for your turn to speak, genuinely engage with what the other person is saying. Demonstrate empathy and understanding by paraphrasing their points, asking clarifying questions, and validating their experiences. By showing that you value their perspective and are truly interested in what they have to say, you can quickly build rapport and likability.

Find Common Ground: Look for commonalities and shared interests that you can bond over with the other person. Whether it's a shared hobby, passion, or experience, finding common ground can create an instant connection and foster a sense of camaraderie. By emphasizing shared values and experiences, you can build bridges across differences and cultivate mutual likability.

Demonstrate Empathy and Understanding: Show empathy and understanding towards the experiences and perspectives of others, particularly those who may be marginalized or underrepresented. Take the time to listen to their stories, validate their feelings, and acknowledge their struggles. By demonstrating empathy and understanding, you can create a sense of trust and comfort that makes others feel valued and respected.

Be Authentic and Genuine: Authenticity is key to building genuine connections with others. Be true to yourself and your values, and avoid trying to be someone you're not in an attempt to impress others. People are drawn to authenticity and sincerity, and they can quickly sense when someone is being insincere or inauthentic. By being genuine and authentic in your interactions, you can cultivate instant likability and build meaningful relationships based on trust and mutual respect.

Smile and Maintain Positive Body Language: A warm smile and positive body language can go a long way in making others feel comfortable and at ease in your presence. Smile genuinely and maintain open and inviting body language, such as making eye contact, nodding in agreement, and leaning slightly towards the other person. These subtle cues signal friendliness and approachability, making it easier for others to like and connect with you.

Show Appreciation and Gratitude:

Express appreciation and gratitude towards others for their contributions, ideas, and perspectives. Take the time to acknowledge their efforts and recognize their strengths and accomplishments. By showing appreciation and gratitude, you can make others feel valued and appreciated, fostering a sense of goodwill and likability.

Be Open-Minded and Flexible: Approach interactions with an open mind and a willingness to consider different perspectives and ideas. Avoid being judgmental or dismissive towards others' viewpoints, even if they differ from your own. Instead, embrace curiosity and openness, and be willing to learn from others' experiences and insights. By demonstrating openness and flexibility, you can create an inclusive and welcoming environment that encourages others to like and connect with you.

Practice Humility and Humbleness: Humility is a powerful trait that can instantly endear you to others. Acknowledge your own strengths and accomplishments, but also be humble about them. Avoid boasting or seeking attention, and instead, focus on lifting others up and celebrating their successes. People are drawn to individuals who are humble and down-to-earth, as it creates an atmosphere of equality and mutual respect.

Offer Help and Support: Show genuine concern for the well-being of others by offering your help and support whenever possible. Whether it's lending a listening ear, providing practical assistance, or offering words of encouragement, demonstrating your willingness to support others can quickly earn you their trust and admiration. By being a source of support and encouragement, you can cultivate instant likability and build strong, lasting relationships.

Practice Empowerment: Empowerment involves recognizing and affirming the inherent worth and agency of others. Instead of trying to assert control or dominance in interactions, strive to empower others to express themselves and pursue their goals. Actively seek out opportunities to uplift and amplify the voices of those who may be marginalized or overlooked. By empowering others, you not only cultivate likability but also contribute to a more inclusive and equitable community.

Maintain a Positive Attitude:

Positivity is contagious, and maintaining a positive attitude can quickly make you more likable to those around you. Approach interactions with optimism and enthusiasm, and try to find the silver lining in every situation. Avoid dwelling on negativity or complaining excessively, as this can dampen the mood and turn others away. By radiating positivity, you can create a welcoming and uplifting environment that draws others towards you.

Be a Good Listener: Actively listen to others and show genuine interest in their thoughts, feelings, and experiences. Avoid interrupting or dominating the conversation, and instead, give others the space to express themselves fully. Practice empathy and compassion in your interactions, and strive to understand things from the other person's perspective. By being a good listener, you demonstrate respect and consideration for others, which can quickly earn you their admiration and respect.

Show Vulnerability: Vulnerability is a sign of strength, not weakness, and sharing your vulnerabilities with others can help to foster deeper connections and trust. Don't be afraid to let your guard down and show your authentic self to others. Share your struggles, fears, and insecurities, and allow others to see the real you. By showing vulnerability, you create an atmosphere of authenticity and intimacy that can quickly endear you to others.

Celebrate Diversity: Embrace and celebrate diversity in all its forms. Recognize the unique perspectives, experiences, and identities that each individual brings to the table. Rather than seeking to homogenize or assimilate others, celebrate the richness and complexity of human diversity. Show genuine interest in learning about different cultures, backgrounds, and traditions, and actively seek out opportunities to engage with diverse communities. By celebrating diversity, you demonstrate inclusivity and respect for others' identities, which can quickly earn you admiration and respect.

Express Gratitude: Expressing gratitude is a powerful way to cultivate instant likability and strengthen relationships. Take the time to acknowledge and appreciate the contributions of others, whether big or small. Express gratitude through sincere thank-you notes, verbal affirmations, or acts of kindness. By expressing gratitude, you demonstrate humility and appreciation for the efforts of others, which can foster feelings of goodwill and connection.

Be Approachable: Cultivate an approachable demeanor that makes others feel comfortable and at ease in your presence. Smile warmly, make eye contact, and maintain an open and inviting body language. Avoid appearing aloof or unapproachable, and instead, convey warmth and friendliness in your interactions. By being approachable, you create an atmosphere of openness and accessibility that encourages others to engage with you.

Seek Feedback and Input: Be open to receiving feedback and input from others, and actively seek out opportunities to learn and grow. Welcome constructive criticism as an opportunity for self-improvement, and be willing to admit when you've made a mistake. Show humility and openness in accepting feedback, and take proactive steps to address any areas for improvement. By seeking feedback and input, you demonstrate a willingness to listen and learn from others, which can enhance your likability and credibility.

Practice Empathy in Action: Demonstrate empathy through your actions by taking the time to understand and address the needs and concerns of others. Offer practical assistance and support to those who may be struggling or in need, and be willing to lend a helping hand whenever possible. Show compassion and kindness towards others, and strive to make a positive difference in their lives. By practicing empathy in action, you demonstrate genuine care and concern for others, which can quickly endear you to them.

Be Authentic and Consistent: Authenticity and consistency are key to building trust and credibility with others. Be true to yourself and your values, and avoid pretending to be someone you're not. Consistently demonstrate integrity and honesty in your words and actions, and strive to live up to your commitments. By being authentic and consistent, you build a reputation for reliability and trustworthiness, which can enhance your likability and credibility in the eyes of others.

Show Respect and Courtesy: Treat others with respect and courtesy in all your interactions, regardless of their background or position. Be mindful of your words and actions, and avoid speaking or behaving in ways that may be hurtful or disrespectful. Show appreciation for others' time and contributions, and be considerate of their feelings and boundaries. By showing respect and courtesy, you create a positive and respectful atmosphere that fosters likability and mutual respect.

In conclusion, cultivating instant likability is about embodying qualities such as empathy, authenticity, gratitude, approachability, and respect in your interactions with others. By practicing these principles within the context of "Never Divide the Disparity," you can quickly build rapport and connection with those around you, fostering a sense of unity, understanding, and mutual appreciation. As we continue on this journey, let us strive to cultivate meaningful relationships and communities grounded in empathy, respect, and solidarity.

9 EMBRACING CONSTRUCTIVE CRITICISM WITH COMPASSION AND UNDERSTANDING

Criticism, when delivered thoughtfully and constructively, can be a powerful tool for growth and improvement. However, in the pursuit of equity and justice encapsulated by the title "Never Divide the Disparity," it's essential to approach criticism with compassion, empathy, and understanding. This chapter explores strategies for giving and receiving criticism in a way that fosters unity, respect, and mutual appreciation.

Focus on Solutions, Not Blame: When delivering criticism, focus on identifying solutions rather than assigning blame. Instead of criticizing someone for their mistakes or shortcomings, offer constructive feedback that highlights areas for improvement and suggests actionable steps for addressing them. By framing criticism as an opportunity for growth and learning, rather than as a personal attack, you can create a more positive and productive dialogue.

Use Compassionate Language: Choose your words carefully when delivering criticism, and strive to use language that is respectful, empathetic, and compassionate. Avoid harsh or judgmental language that may cause the other person to feel defensive or attacked. Instead, use "I" statements to express your concerns and feelings, and frame your criticism in a way that acknowledges the other person's perspective and experiences.

Offer Specific and Actionable Feedback: When giving criticism, be specific about the behaviors or actions that you are addressing, and provide concrete examples to illustrate your points. Avoid vague or general criticisms that may leave the other person feeling confused or overwhelmed. Instead, offer actionable feedback that clearly outlines the steps that the other person can take to address the issue and improve.

Encourage Dialogue and Collaboration: Approach criticism as an opportunity for dialogue and collaboration, rather than as a one-sided lecture. Invite the other person to share their perspective and feelings on the matter, and be open to hearing their side of the story. Collaborate on finding solutions together, and brainstorm ways to address the issue in a way that respects everyone's needs and concerns.

Focus on Growth and Development: Frame criticism as a catalyst for growth and development, rather than as a punishment or condemnation. Emphasize the potential for learning and improvement that comes from receiving feedback, and encourage the other person to see criticism as an opportunity for self-reflection and personal growth. By reframing criticism in a positive light, you can help others to approach it with a more open and receptive mindset.

Express Appreciation and Recognition: Whenever possible, express appreciation and recognition for the other person's efforts and contributions, even when delivering criticism. Acknowledge their strengths and accomplishments, and affirm your belief in their ability to overcome challenges and succeed. By balancing criticism with appreciation, you can help to maintain a positive and supportive relationship with the other person.

Be Open to Receiving Criticism: Just as important as giving criticism thoughtfully and compassionately is being open to receiving criticism in the same manner. Approach criticism with an open mind and a willingness to learn and grow from feedback. Resist the urge to become defensive or dismissive, and instead, listen actively to the other person's perspective and consider their feedback with sincerity and humility.

Practice Self-Reflection and Improvement: Use criticism as an opportunity for self-reflection and self-improvement. Instead of dwelling on negative feelings or becoming defensive, take constructive criticism as an opportunity to identify areas for growth and development. Consider how you can use feedback to become a better communicator, collaborator, and advocate for equity and justice. By approaching criticism with a growth mindset, you can turn even the most challenging feedback into an opportunity for personal and professional development.

Seek Consent for Critique: Before offering criticism, seek consent from the individual you wish to provide feedback to. Respect their boundaries and readiness to receive feedback, as not everyone may be open to critique at all times. By asking for permission to provide feedback, you demonstrate respect for their autonomy and create a more receptive environment for constructive dialogue.

Offer Praise Alongside Criticism: When providing criticism, balance it with genuine praise and recognition for the individual's strengths and accomplishments. Highlighting their positive qualities alongside areas for improvement helps to maintain their confidence and motivation. It also fosters a supportive atmosphere where individuals feel valued and encouraged to continue their growth journey.

Provide Context and Intent: Clearly communicate the context and intent behind your criticism to avoid misunderstandings or hurt feelings. Explain why the feedback is being given and how it aligns with shared goals and values. This helps the individual understand that the criticism is coming from a place of care and commitment to their development, rather than from a desire to belittle or demean them.

Encourage Self-Reflection: Empower individuals to engage in self-reflection by prompting them to consider how the feedback resonates with their own experiences and aspirations. Encourage them to explore the underlying reasons behind their behaviors or actions and to identify strategies for personal growth and improvement. By fostering self-awareness and agency, you support individuals in taking ownership of their development journey.

Follow Up and Check-In: After providing criticism, follow up with the individual to check in on their progress and offer continued support and guidance. Acknowledge any positive changes or efforts they have made in response to the feedback and offer encouragement to keep moving forward. Regular check-ins demonstrate your ongoing commitment to their development and reinforce the importance of constructive feedback as a tool for growth.

Model Vulnerability and Growth: Lead by example by being open about your own areas for improvement and growth. Share stories of times when you received constructive criticism and how you used it to learn and develop. By modeling vulnerability and a growth mindset, you create a culture where feedback is valued and seen as a natural part of the learning process.

Create a Feedback Culture: Foster a

culture of continuous feedback and learning within your organization or community. Encourage open communication and transparency, and provide opportunities for individuals to give and receive feedback regularly. By normalizing feedback as a constructive and supportive practice, you create an environment where everyone feels empowered to contribute to each other's growth and development.

Acknowledge Effort and Progress: Recognize and acknowledge the efforts and progress made by individuals in response to criticism. Celebrate small victories and milestones along their journey of growth and improvement. By affirming their progress, you reinforce their confidence and motivation to continue striving for excellence.

Normalize Imperfection: Encourage a culture that embraces imperfection and views mistakes as opportunities for learning and growth. Normalize the idea that nobody is perfect and that making errors is a natural part of the human experience. By destigmatizing failure and promoting a growth mindset, you create an environment where individuals feel safe to take risks and learn from their experiences.

Offer Supportive Resources: Provide individuals with access to resources and support systems that can aid them in addressing areas for improvement. This could include mentoring, coaching, training programs, or professional development opportunities. By equipping individuals with the tools and resources they need to succeed, you empower them to take ownership of their growth and development journey.

Encourage Peer-to-Peer Feedback: Foster a culture of peer-to-peer feedback where individuals feel empowered to provide constructive criticism to their peers in a respectful and supportive manner. Encourage peer mentoring and coaching relationships where individuals can learn from each other's experiences and perspectives. By promoting collaboration and mutual support, you create a community where everyone plays a role in each other's growth and development.

Reflect and Adapt: Continuously reflect on your own approach to giving and receiving criticism and be willing to adapt and evolve as needed. Solicit feedback from others on your communication style and effectiveness in delivering criticism. Use this feedback as an opportunity for self-improvement and growth. By modeling a commitment to continuous learning and adaptation, you set a positive example for others and create a culture that values self-reflection and growth.

Celebrate Learning Moments: Embrace criticism as a learning opportunity and celebrate the insights gained from constructive feedback. Encourage individuals to share their experiences of receiving criticism and the lessons they learned from it. By reframing criticism as a valuable source of wisdom and growth, you cultivate a culture that values continuous learning and development.

In conclusion, navigating criticism within the framework of "Never Divide the Disparity" requires a multifaceted approach that prioritizes compassion, empathy, and growth. By acknowledging effort and progress, normalizing imperfection, offering supportive resources, encouraging peer-to-peer feedback, reflecting and adapting, and celebrating learning moments, we can create a culture where criticism is embraced as a catalyst for personal and collective development. As we continue on this journey, let us strive to cultivate a culture of compassion and understanding where everyone feels empowered to learn, grow, and thrive.

10 EMBRACING UNCERTAINTY AND HUMILITY

In the pursuit of equity and justice encapsulated by the title "Never Divide the Disparity," it is crucial to recognize the limitations of our own perspectives and the complexity of the issues we seek to address. Chapter Ten explores the importance of embracing uncertainty and humility in our efforts to promote equity and justice.

Recognizing the Complexity of Social Issues: Many social issues, such as poverty, inequality, and discrimination, are multifaceted and deeply rooted in systemic factors. It's essential to acknowledge the complexity of these issues and recognize that there are no easy solutions or quick fixes. Embracing uncertainty means being willing to grapple with the complexity of social issues without oversimplifying or minimizing their significance.

Valuing Diverse Perspectives: Embracing uncertainty involves acknowledging that there are multiple perspectives and experiences that contribute to our understanding of social issues. It requires humility in recognizing that our own perspectives may be limited and that we can learn from the insights and experiences of others. Valuing diverse perspectives allows us to approach complex issues with greater nuance and empathy.

Cultivating a Growth Mindset:

Embracing uncertainty means adopting a growth mindset, characterized by a willingness to learn, adapt, and grow from our experiences. Instead of seeing uncertainty as a sign of weakness or incompetence, we can view it as an opportunity for growth and self-improvement. Cultivating a growth mindset allows us to approach challenges with resilience and optimism, knowing that we can learn and evolve over time.

Engaging in Continuous Learning: Embracing uncertainty requires a commitment to ongoing learning and self-reflection. It involves being open to new ideas, perspectives, and information, even when it challenges our existing beliefs or assumptions. Engaging in continuous learning allows us to expand our understanding of social issues and develop more effective strategies for promoting equity and justice.

Practicing Humility in Advocacy: Embracing uncertainty means approaching advocacy with humility and a willingness to listen and learn from others. It involves recognizing that we may not have all the answers and that there is always more to learn. Practicing humility in advocacy allows us to build more authentic relationships with those we seek to support and advocate for, fostering trust and collaboration.

Seeking Feedback and Collaboration: Embracing uncertainty involves seeking feedback and collaboration from others in our efforts to promote equity and justice. It means being open to constructive criticism and diverse perspectives, and actively seeking out opportunities for collaboration with individuals and organizations that share our goals. Seeking feedback and collaboration allows us to leverage the collective wisdom and expertise of others, leading to more impactful and sustainable outcomes.

Embracing Failure as a Learning Opportunity: Embracing uncertainty means being willing to take risks and embrace failure as a natural part of the learning process. It involves reframing failure as a valuable learning opportunity rather than as a reflection of our worth or competence. Embracing failure allows us to push past our comfort zones and innovate new approaches to addressing social issues.

Maintaining a Sense of Curiosity and Wonder: Embracing uncertainty involves maintaining a sense of curiosity and wonder about the world around us. It means approaching social issues with a sense of humility and awe, recognizing that there is always more to learn and discover. Maintaining a sense of curiosity and wonder allows us to stay open to new ideas and perspectives, fueling our passion for promoting equity and justice.

Navigating Ambiguity with Grace: Embracing uncertainty also entails navigating ambiguity with grace and resilience. It requires being comfortable with ambiguity and complexity, even when faced with situations that lack clear-cut solutions or outcomes. Navigating ambiguity with grace involves maintaining composure and adaptability in the face of uncertainty, trusting in our ability to navigate challenges and make informed decisions.

Building Bridges Across Differences: Embracing uncertainty involves recognizing that progress towards equity and justice may not always follow a linear path. It requires a willingness to engage with individuals and communities with diverse perspectives, backgrounds, and experiences. Building bridges across differences means embracing the uncertainty that comes with navigating diverse viewpoints and finding common ground amidst complexity.

Challenging Assumptions and Biases: Embracing uncertainty requires challenging our own assumptions and biases, as well as those embedded within societal structures and systems. It involves confronting the uncertainty that arises from acknowledging the ways in which our own perspectives may be shaped by privilege, bias, or limited understanding. By interrogating assumptions and biases, we create space for more inclusive and equitable dialogue and action.

Embracing the Unpredictability of Change: Embracing uncertainty also means accepting the unpredictability of change and transformation. It requires acknowledging that progress towards equity and justice may unfold in unexpected ways and may be influenced by factors beyond our control. Embracing the unpredictability of change means remaining adaptable and resilient in the face of uncertainty, trusting in our ability to navigate change and respond effectively to emerging challenges.

Honoring Indigenous Ways of Knowing: Embracing uncertainty

involves recognizing and honoring Indigenous ways of knowing that prioritize interconnectedness, reciprocity, and humility. It requires acknowledging the limitations of Western-centric knowledge systems and embracing the uncertainty that comes with integrating diverse ways of knowing into our understanding of equity and justice. By centering Indigenous perspectives, we can navigate uncertainty with greater humility and respect for the interconnectedness of all life.

Fostering Resilience in the Face of Adversity: Embracing uncertainty requires fostering resilience in the face of adversity and setbacks. It involves cultivating a sense of inner strength and determination that allows us to persevere in the pursuit of equity and justice, even when faced with uncertainty and challenges. Fostering resilience means embracing uncertainty as an opportunity for growth and transformation, rather than as a barrier to progress.

Cultivating Trust and Collaboration: Embracing uncertainty also entails cultivating trust and collaboration among individuals and communities working towards equity and justice. It requires creating spaces for dialogue, collaboration, and collective action that embrace uncertainty as a natural part of the process. By fostering trust and collaboration, we can navigate uncertainty with greater collective wisdom and strength, working together towards shared goals.

In conclusion, embracing uncertainty is essential in the pursuit of equity and justice. By navigating ambiguity with grace, building bridges across differences, challenging assumptions and biases, embracing the unpredictability of change, honoring Indigenous ways of knowing, fostering resilience, and cultivating trust and collaboration, we can navigate uncertainty with greater humility, resilience, and effectiveness. As we continue on this journey, let us embrace uncertainty as an opportunity for growth and transformation, knowing that it is through embracing the unknown that we can create a more just and equitable world.

Setting Boundaries

In the pursuit of equity and justice encapsulated by the title "Never Divide the Disparity," it's crucial to establish and uphold boundaries that promote fairness, respect, and inclusivity. This final chapter explores the importance of setting boundaries in our efforts to bridge disparities and create a more equitable society.

Defining Personal Boundaries: Setting personal boundaries is essential for maintaining self-respect and ensuring that our needs and values are honored. It involves clearly defining what is acceptable and unacceptable in our interactions with others, and communicating those boundaries assertively and respectfully. Defining personal boundaries allows us to protect our mental, emotional, and physical well-being, and fosters a sense of agency and autonomy.

Respecting Others' Boundaries: Just as important as setting our own boundaries is respecting the boundaries of others. It requires listening attentively to their needs and preferences, and refraining from actions or behaviors that violate their boundaries. Respecting others' boundaries fosters trust, respect, and mutual understanding in our relationships, and creates a supportive and inclusive environment where everyone feels valued and respected.

Establishing Boundaries in Advocacy: Setting boundaries is also crucial in advocacy work, where we may encounter challenging situations or individuals who push against our values and principles. It involves establishing clear guidelines for engagement and communication, and being willing to assert our boundaries when they are crossed. Establishing boundaries in advocacy ensures that we can advocate effectively while also maintaining our integrity and well-being.

Creating Inclusive Spaces: Setting boundaries is an essential aspect of creating inclusive and equitable spaces where everyone feels safe, respected, and valued. It involves establishing ground rules and norms that promote respect, empathy, and understanding, and enforcing those boundaries consistently and equitably. Creating inclusive spaces requires us to challenge behaviors or attitudes that perpetuate discrimination or marginalization, and to actively work towards creating environments where everyone can thrive.

Navigating Power Dynamics: Setting boundaries becomes particularly important when navigating power dynamics in relationships or communities. It requires us to be aware of how power imbalances can impact our interactions and to assert our boundaries assertively and confidently, even in the face of resistance or pushback. Navigating power dynamics with boundaries ensures that everyone's voice is heard and respected, regardless of their position or status.

Communicating Boundaries Effectively: Setting boundaries effectively requires clear and assertive communication. It involves expressing our needs, preferences, and limits in a direct and respectful manner, and being willing to enforce those boundaries if they are violated. Communicating boundaries effectively fosters mutual respect and understanding in our relationships, and creates a foundation of trust and accountability that allows for healthy and constructive interactions.

Reinforcing Boundaries Consistently: Setting boundaries is an ongoing process that requires reinforcement and maintenance over time. It involves being vigilant in recognizing when our boundaries are being tested or violated, and taking action to assert and reinforce those boundaries as needed. Reinforcing boundaries consistently sends a clear message that our values and well-being are non-negotiable, and fosters a culture of respect and accountability in our relationships and communities.

Seeking Support and Accountability: Setting boundaries can be challenging, especially in situations where we may face resistance or backlash. It's essential to seek support and accountability from trusted friends, colleagues, or mentors who can provide guidance and encouragement as we navigate boundary-setting. Seeking support and accountability helps us stay true to our values and priorities, and empowers us to assert our boundaries with confidence and conviction.

In conclusion, setting boundaries is essential in the pursuit of equity and justice. By defining personal boundaries, respecting others' boundaries, establishing boundaries in advocacy, creating inclusive spaces, navigating power dynamics, communicating boundaries effectively, reinforcing boundaries consistently, and seeking support and accountability, we can create a more just and equitable society where everyone's needs and values are honored and respected. As we continue on this journey, let us uphold the principles of "Never Divide the Disparity" by setting and respecting boundaries that promote fairness, respect, and inclusivity for all.

Reflecting on Boundary Impact: It's crucial to reflect on the impact of boundaries on ourselves and others. We must consider how our boundaries may affect those around us and be open to adjusting them as necessary to promote fairness and inclusivity. Reflecting on boundary impact allows us to ensure that our boundaries align with our values of equity and justice and contribute to creating a more harmonious and respectful environment for everyone.

Embracing Boundary Flexibility: While boundaries are important for maintaining our well-being and integrity, it's also essential to embrace flexibility when necessary. Sometimes, rigid adherence to boundaries may hinder collaboration or impede progress towards equity and justice. Embracing boundary flexibility allows us to adapt to changing circumstances and find creative solutions that prioritize the greater good while still respecting individual needs and boundaries.

Empowering Others to Set Boundaries: As advocates for equity and justice, we have a responsibility to empower others to set and assert their own boundaries. This involves creating a culture that values and respects boundaries and providing support and encouragement to individuals as they navigate boundary-setting in their own lives. Empowering others to set boundaries helps to create a more equitable and compassionate society where everyone's autonomy and dignity are upheld.

Celebrating Boundary Successes: Finally, it's essential to celebrate the successes and achievements that result from boundary-setting efforts. Whether it's fostering healthier relationships, creating more inclusive spaces, or advancing progress towards equity and justice, every step taken to set and respect boundaries is worthy of celebration. Celebrating boundary successes reinforces the importance of boundary-setting in our collective efforts to create positive change and inspires others to continue advocating for fairness and respect.

Conclusion:

In conclusion, the principle of "Never Divide the Disparity" underscores the importance of setting and respecting boundaries in our pursuit of equity and justice. By defining personal boundaries, respecting others' boundaries, establishing boundaries in advocacy, creating inclusive spaces, navigating power dynamics, communicating boundaries effectively, reinforcing boundaries consistently, seeking support and accountability, reflecting on boundary impact, embracing boundary flexibility, empowering others to set boundaries, and celebrating boundary successes, we can create a more equitable and compassionate society where everyone's needs and values are honored and respected. As we continue on this journey, let us uphold the principles of fairness, respect, and inclusivity by setting and respecting boundaries that promote equity and justice for all. Together, we can build a world where disparities are bridged, and unity and solidarity prevail.

ABOUT THE AUTHOR

Vana Hendy is a seasoned wordsmith with a passion for storytelling that has captivated readers around the world. Born and raised in Nigeria, Vana Hendy discovered the magic of words at an early age, weaving tales that transported readers to fantastical realms and stirred their imaginations.

With a degree in Marketing from Coal City University , Vana Hendy combines a strongacademic foundation with a natural flair for creative expression. This unique blend of knowledge and creativity is evident in herability to craft narratives that are both intellectually stimulating and emotionally resonant.

Vana Hendy has a diverse literary palette, having penned works spanning various genres, from gripping mystery novels to heartwarming romance stories.

she believes in the transformative power of storytelling, using words to inspire, entertain, and provoke thought.